STREET ACTION

STREET ACTION
STYLE AND POWER ON MAIN STREET USA

David Jacobs, Mike Key
& Andrew Morland

OSPREY
AUTOMOTIVE

Published in 1991 by Osprey Publishing Limited, 59 Grosvenor Street, London W1X 9DA

© David Jacobs, Mike Key, Andrew Morland, 1991

British Library Cataloguing in Publication Data

Jacobs, David 1952–
Street action.
1. United States. Vehicles
I. Title II. Key, Mike
III. Morland, Andrew
629.0460973

ISBN 1-85532-139-4

Compiled, edited and designed by Roger Chesneau

Phototypeset in the UK by Typesetters (Birmingham) Ltd

Printed in Hong Kong

The images in this book come from the work of David Jacobs, Mike Key and Andrew Morland. Their outstanding photographs have been seen in *American Tow Trucks* (David Jacobs); *American Trucks* (David Jacobs); *American Trucks 2* (David Jacobs); *Custom and Race Trucks* (David Jacobs); *Truck Racing* (Mike Key); *Tri-Chevy* (Mike Key); *Street Machines* (Andrew Morland); *Lamborghini* (Andrew Morland); and *Off Road* (Andrew Morland). All these titles are published by Osprey in its Colour Series.

Picture credits
David Jacobs: pages 2, 7–77, 79, 82, 84–87, 89–94
Mike Key: pages 6, 78, 80–83, 88–89, 95, 132–171
Andrew Morland: pages 4, 96–131, 172–224

CONTENTS

INTRODUCTION

America has always been tremendously creative with the automobile. Although the first cars were made in Europe, it was the United States that showed the world how to build cars that everyone could afford. Yet, right from the beginning, the USA put style on the streets.

Variety and individuality distinguish the American automobile. Detroit has a greater number of strong manufacturers than France, Germany and Britain combined. Cadillac, Buick, Ford, Pontiac, Mercury, Chrysler, Oldsmobile, Dodge, Lincoln, Plymouth and Chevrolet lead the roster of leading brands. Each offers a bewildering number of models. And for each model there is an even greater selection of options. It is surprising that there are no two vehicles alike coming from the 'Big Three' manufacturers.

Add the cars built today to those that saw better days and you begin to understand why America has so much to choose from and why its streets are such a carnival. De Soto, Hudson, Studebaker, Willys, AMC and even Packard machines are still around in enough numbers to serve as a foundation for anyone who wants to customize an automobile.

And what about the customizers? The United States gave the word to the world. The ordinary driver, with just a few hundred dollars, can make any car individual to him or her and like no other. It could be with just a simple all-over paint job in a novel colour

BELOW Around 185,000 Bel Air Sport Coupes were produced in 1955. The number plate shows what this owner thinks of his car.

mixed by the local wizard with a spraygun, or it could be a garage project that takes years and infinite pains.

Many of the finest auto-stylists started in a modest way messing around with cars—nothing elaborate, just a place to work out back, a set of regular tools and a desire to stand apart. While the others were goofing off, they were doing something practical. Often, friends came around and asked for a little help, and that was the start of a thriving business.

From high school senior to President there is no need to have a 'me-too-mobile'. And the same goes for trucks. America lives by its roads, and the people who earn their living with the wreckers that serve the local community, or go coast-to-coast with their rigs costing over $100,000, all personalize their vehicles. Sometimes they just have their names painted in fancy letters on the driver's door. But often they go the whole route by selecting every item on the bill from the cab frame to the chrome top on the stack.

No wonder the USA invented custom trucks, truck racing and the sheer spectacle of monster machines crushing trade-ins heading for the junk yard. Hot-rodding was another American invention, along with street machines which were good enough to put in 'pro' performances on the quarter-mile drag strip. Nowhere on the globe can you see so many individually engineered cars with world class potential.

Even off road, a 4 × 4 built in the United States has a quite distinct appearance. From the go-anywhere 'Jeep' to the luxury leisure cruiser, you can tell at a glance that here is a vehicle which is rugged and built for fun.

Overall, no other nation has so many different types of vehicle, or the means to let an individual have so much choice.

BELOW In for a cent, in for a dollar. Customize your truck and then match its hue on your Mk V Lincoln Continental—just like Bob Wilson's *Ironsides*.

CUSTOM TRUCKS

America's Interstate Highway system covers the country from the cool, wooded mountains of New England to the broiling heat of Death Valley. The folk that drive the big rigs are as tough and as varied as the country they love.

Custom trucks are custom-built throughout. An owner specifies exactly what he wants, from the tyres to the fancy paint job. He's going to spend a lot of time behind the wheel so every detail has got to be perfect.

The wrong choice of cab length, engine power, gearbox, suspension set-up, fuel system, and a thousand other factors can make a good truck a nightmare. Truckers take pride in knowing what they want and how to have it built right.

But the public pays more notice to a rig's paintwork and chrome. The sight of a well turned out Kenworth, White, Mack or International Harvester is exciting. And the boys that run General Motors, Ford and Peterbilt reckon they do even better. It is a fierce contest.

A lot of thought goes into these numerous coats of ground colour and pure, clear lacquer. It costs thousands of dollars to paint a truck properly. But the complex designs, the elaborate signwriting and the powerful stripes are more than just decoration. They proclaim an owner's fiercely defended rights and independence. It's his money, and nobody is going to make him become just another conformist like the characters he passes in their offices when he is out on the Interstate heading for a spot three days away.

LEFT Paintwork inspired by hot rodders from way back highlights this handsome Peterbilt conventional and low-loader. This is a working rig.

ABOVE *Wild Cherry*—a surprisingly unadorned Peterbilt customized with much good taste. Here it sits at the 76 truckstop in Santa Nella, California, known as Andersen's Inn.

BELOW Bob Wilson spent mega-bucks in 1979 to produce this custom winner, *Ironsides*. Conventional KW with sleeper cab provides the base.

ABOVE Fletchoe Diesel Fuel Inc. of Barstow, California, believe in the working custom truck. Show winner everywhere.

BELOW Double trouble—1948 GMC conventional pulling a 1944 Weber flatbed trailer. Another custom show winner.

BELOW Wyoming KW Aerodyne in California, at
Santa Nella. Night trip about to start.

BELOW This 1980 KW Aerodyne of George and Fran
Ulm has everything. They even did their own paint job.

ABOVE We have seen cabovers like this before. But it's still fun.

ABOVE RIGHT Smoke House Meats entered their Freightliner cabover for the Beauty Contest. Could have been a winner.

RIGHT Perfection knows no bounds. This early Peterbilt with double low-loader is a working truck prepped for showing. Known as *Mr Chrome*.

BELOW Bert D. Van Dyk's '48 GMC and '44 Weber reach for the sky.

BOTTOM Kimkris Trucking are still happy to use early GMC conventionals. Not much evidence of CB on the two rigs in the shot.

Ironsides again in all its glory. Little actual modification—just dollars of chrome, paint and lacquer make that shine.

BELOW Only the American exhaust stack can outshine the paintwork. Texan truck in the red sunset.

ABOVE Nearly brand new White Western Star from
Kenworth. No. 53 in the fleet, number 1 for colour.

ABOVE Parked at a Beauty Contest at Bakersfield.
Superb double grain tanker trailer, Peterbilt up front.

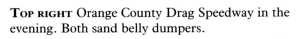

TOP RIGHT Orange County Drag Speedway in the evening. Both sand belly dumpers.

RIGHT Handsome paint on this red/purple Peterbilt rig. Special air conditioner for the cab.

ABOVE Snow White is right for this fridge-rig. Conventional in every way, this Peterbilt still looks striking.

RIGHT Six cabovers lined up for judging. Another Bob Wilson truck from Montebello, California, this time a Kenworth heads the line before a White Freightliner.

RIGHT Even though it's a custom show truck this early Ford conventional does a good day's work five days a week. It's Kern County show weekend today. 'Old can be goodie too'.

Miss Debbie, 'Longhorn' Pete.

ABOVE Night light.

ABOVE Rare Western Star with over 475 horsepower!

RIGHT Gold waterfall: California sunset on a reefer.

FAR RIGHT Bill Reisch wanted real stained glass windows in his sleeper cab. In Utah they were no problem to find. Nice touch.

BELOW Night insects.

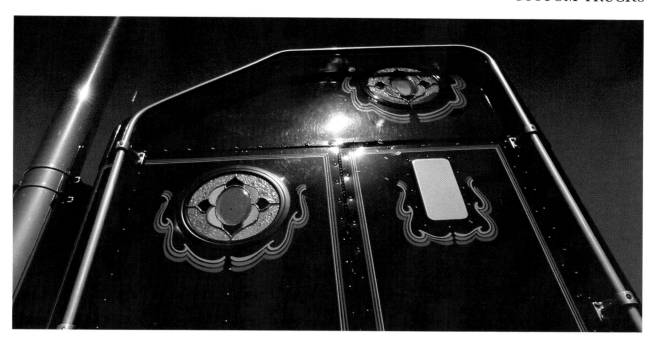

ABOVE Knuckle-duster your exhaust stack. Just bullet studs, for decoration only.

Over 400 horsepower marked for this black chrome
beauty.

RIGHT Dressing up for the truck custom show goes for everyone. Jan Prentice makes adjustments to *Motion Lotion*.

BELOW *101* doesn't seem a high enough number for this driver/truck combination. Kellie Donahue and Kenworth gas tanker.

BELOW RIGHT 'If you can't show it, blow it'. Polished boots show proper dedication.

ABOVE Rare Western Star from the White Truck Group International. Crucifix lights.

TOP RIGHT Tidy.

RIGHT No, not real spoke wheels on a truck but the next best thing. These gold wires are but inserts carefully clipped into the wheel rim.

Left Fantasy mural cab-back in a style more often seen on motorcycle tanks.

ABOVE Funky art for a truck flap.

LEFT Pack of Mack.

BELOW Anatomy out of perspective.

TOW TRUCKS

Big or small, tow trucks have a tough job. The easy recovery from the side of the highway is the exception. Trucks, cars, buses and special-use vehicles all have a habit of ending up in awkward places. It takes skill, and raw courage, to drag a tanker full of gas out of a swamp, or rescue a trailer-load of panic-stricken livestock.

And a tow truck has got to be ready at all times. It may stand by for long hours, even days, but as soon as the ignition key is turned the engine has got to deliver full power.

LEFT Nice colour coordinated Kenworth conventional. Note TRAA (Towing and Recovery Association of America) symbol on trucker's shirt.

BELOW Wrecker controls.

LEFT Bert's Peterbilt sparkles in the midday sun outside the New Orleans superdome.

BELOW LEFT Unusual cabover International Transtar wrecker at Castaic, north of San Fernando.

BELOW Sparkling chrome on a working 1985 Freightliner. Note the rectangular headlamps.

Above Whiter than white, except it's an Autocar!

Below Careful detailing on Bambarger's 1967 International with a Holmes 16-ton wrecker.

Right A distinctive red and yellow Mack conventional ready to go.

Below right Outstanding Gimmie conventional. Note duo-tone paintwork.

Immaculate Holmes 750 wrecker lifts a beaten-up
Ford conventional.

ABOVE This Dragon Wagon has real fire. The truckers' gear is standard.

ABOVE RIGHT AND RIGHT Not much standard about the finish on this beauty.

BELOW Big wrecker with Hubbard Anchor—extending boom. Neat.

RIGHT Toolkit.

BELOW RIGHT Beat this. There's no place like Holmes.

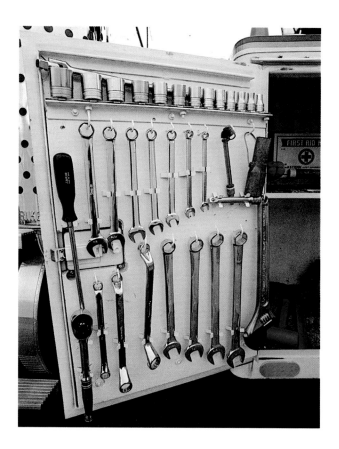

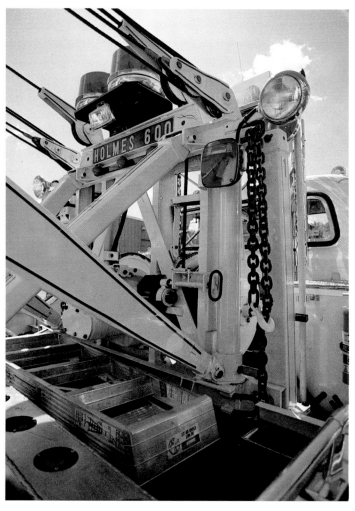

ABOVE Small is beautiful. Note the safety straps on this Century telescopic lifting bar.

BELOW Yellow carpet treatment.

RIGHT A classic Mack. This 1959 B73 has 200,000 miles on the clock.

BELOW RIGHT Not even the chrome outshines the paintwork on the Aerodyne Kenworth.

LEFT No tangling with the nudge bar on this unusual International Paystar 5000.

BELOW FAR LEFT Class glass.

BELOW LEFT Showboat, show truck.

BELOW Basking in the applause—a gleaming International.

LEFT Neat for the street.

BELOW LEFT This is Dallas country.

BELOW Unusual Autocar twin-steer wrecker. As effective at the drags as at dragging.

A new slant on home removals. An Allied Van Lines International cabover is salvaged by Kelly McKnight's Mack conventional wrecker under a blazing Texan sky. This was an easy one – next call might be a plane in a swamp.

BELOW Riding in style—a Chevy carrying a Chevy?

BOTTOM Going to the show in style.

BELOW Big Tow—which way to turn? This eye-catching candy-apple red beauty has independent front and rear steering. It's a 1979 Ford 1-ton with a Challenger single line hydraulic. A 600 horsepower engine fires this superb 'show and go' wrecker.

LEFT Classy black pickup.

BELOW The Western flavour.

TOP Airbrushed glory.

ABOVE AND RIGHT Two ways of looking at it.

TOP RIGHT Reflections.

FAR RIGHT Service with a smile.

76

RACE TRUCKS

Brute power and 'knock 'em dead' style are the twin keys to the race truck kingdom. It is a world of the ever-moving quest for the ultimate.

Engines are anything but stock. It might read Cummins, Caterpillar, Detroit, Ford or GMC on the block, but underneath you will find cams with wild grinds, race pistons, 'bullet-proof' crankshafts and a host of components made from hi-tech alloys to special order.

Gearboxes have 'trick' ratios. These are absolutely vital for trucks which compete in closed arenas. With such short straights, acceleration has to match a race car's. No mean feat when your all-up weight can be 8,000 lb or more.

The transmissions are very tough. They have to take the shock of 500 bhp or more coming from the flywheel. If the bellhousing and the other units are not up to the job, the transmission can explode like an aluminium fragmentation grenade.

Wheels and tyres can be a tremendous problem. The hubs have to withstand fantastic stresses, especially when a truck hits a corner at 100 mph. The tyres, too, need to resist bursting pressures of hundreds of pounds per square inch at peak loads.

And if these feats of engineering were not enough, the race trucks have to look immaculate. Sponsors want their names to shine, especially as the sport is becoming very important to cable television.

Racing trucks attract a rare breed of driver. It takes something rather special to power-slide a rig or pull a crowd-pleasing wheelie down a straightaway.

LEFT Johnny Harrera lights the tyres as he launches his 600 bhp Cummins-powered Freightliner down the quarter-mile.

LEFT Ready to launch. A drag-racing Peterbilt conventional on the start line with full staging lanes behind.

BELOW LEFT Wheel-to-wheel racing is common on the American oval tracks. Here the pack is led down the straight by a neat open-wheel White.

BELOW With exhaust stacks trailing twin plumes of diesel smoke, this International sets off on a trip down the quarter-mile.

ABOVE LEFT All racer—stark, smooth and built to win.

LEFT After dark on the dragstrip, the roaring trucks seem even more monstrous. Even oldies can come out to play.

ABOVE A shot from the good old days. A Peterbilt conventional looks the business on a tarmac oval track.

BELOW Dusk falls at the dragstrip and another Mack roars down the quarter-mile.

At speed. No. 97, Mike Adams, qualified second at over 105 mph. The two KWs in front were a little slower.

TOP Anything seems to go in American truck drag racing—including racing heavy-duty wreckers!

ABOVE Cabovers are, however, unusual in track racing. Bill Oke wasn't too fast.

TOP *Big Mack . . .*   **ABOVE** If you can't beat them, smoke them out . . .

RIGHT America's version of the wheelie truck heads skywards. Appropriately, it is powered by a 2000 hp Allison V12 aircraft engine.

BELOW Lean and mean. This stripped and lowered White belches plenty of smoke from its stacks as it accelerates around the track.

BELOW RIGHT Oshkosh wrecker, winner and both *Penthouse* and *Playboy* promoters. Truck is spotless.

89

BELOW Fast motor.

BOTTOM They go for seat belts and roll cages.

RIGHT Colour coordination for Bob Lashley's Lincoln.

BELOW RIGHT Like NASCAR racers, these trucks require window nets for driver safety.

BELOW FAR RIGHT Number 2 for *The Flying Deu2ce*. Racer paint.

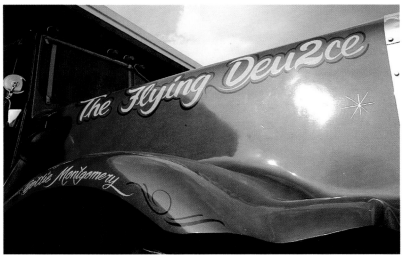

BELOW I got pipes.

BELOW Nerf bars and safety clips for the windscreen.

ABOVE Immaculate diesel with custom paint on the block. It's an Autocar.

ABOVE RIGHT Bright red Detroit Diesel V8 engine, with plenty of plumbing for cooling and for the turbo plus supercharger.

RIGHT Slim Borgudd's turbocharged V8 engine, prepared by West Coast Diesel.

BELOW Starting with an ex-commercial cab and chassis which he picked up for $150, Jerry Yorek from Wantagh, New York, completed this 1975 Chevy LUV in three months flat. After modifying the chassis to accept a Pro Street wheel and tyre combination and a narrowed 9 in. Ford rear, Jerry reinforced it right through to take the strain from a blown 350 small-block. New front panels were added together with a '79 bed, then the whole lot was sprayed in Porsche red lacquer with GM black accent stripes. A new interior, much detailing, and Jerry has got himself one of the toughest *Bloneluv* pick-up trucks on the street.

STREET MACHINES

BELOW AND RIGHT Illinois truck owner/operator Lloyd McVey gets his kicks in this trendy '71 Dodge Challenger. Amongst other things it incorporates a complete Alston chassis and rollcage kit, a Strange Engineering-prepped Dana 60 rear end with ladder bars and Koni coil-over shocks, and a trick lift-off front end. Power is supplied by a blown 426 ci Hemi which has been filled with go-faster goodies like Arias pistons, Keith Black rods, crank and heads, and a Donovan valvetrain. The Dyers-driven supercharger is fed by a pair of Carter carbs and a Crager manifold. Only a fool would challenge this trucker.

ABOVE Jim Porter, a fishing tackle store owner from Springfield, Illinois, spent the best part of three years transforming a $100 '68 VW into this beautiful Baja Bug. While most Bajas are built to take the rough stuff, Jim built his to win trophies and to be seen on the street. In less than a year his efforts have been rewarded with over 20 pots at various shows, including those for Best VW, Best Paint and People's Choice. A cut-above the average 'People's Car', for sure!

BELOW AND RIGHT Think of the most outrageous possible modifications that can be made to a vehicle and you can almost guarantee that someone, somewhere has done it to the ubiquitous VW Bug. The very nature of the Volkswagen makes it the perfect basis for an individual creation, which is why there are so many truly unique VW street machines. Who'd ever suspect that underneath these moulded-together front panels lies a 600-horsepower Chevy V8? Only the eagle-eyed would ever notice the radiator air intake between the front nerf bars. Had the owner refrained from striping the rear end of the car and kept the bodywork totally stock-looking, this would have to be the ultimate 'sleeper' (sheep in wolf's clothing).

A shimmering Metalflake paint scheme makes this '69
Stingray stand out from the crowd, albeit 'out of style'.

ABOVE Post-muscle era Z28 runs a heavy number up front and you can be certain the owner likes to use it.

RIGHT Being an assembly line worker at Ford's Rouge complex in Dearborn, Michigan, it's hardly surprising that Arthur Esper owns two Ford vehicles. One is a 302 Boss Mustang currently under restoration, but the other is slightly *different*: this home-brewed 4 × 4 'English' Ford Thames panel truck. Arthur has successfully amalgamated the cute 1960 body with the all-wheel drive components from a '78 Jeep, thanks to a well-designed home-made frame. Not only that, but he's also managed to squeeze in a turbo'd 2-litre Pinto motor together with its 4-speed trans. A one-off adapter plate was needed to mate the latter with the 4-wheel drive transfer case. Arthur's neat little rig delivers a regular 28 mpg on the street but, and quote, 'It's really too good to take out in the woods'. Most off-beat 4-wheel drive combos are straightforward body swaps made to look as outrageous as possible with the addition of monster tyres. Arthur's Ford on the other hand has been tailor-made to look as if it came from the factory that way—disregarding the Candy Red custom paint job and Walt Disney-inspired artwork, of course.

LEFT Danny Ramsey's '67 Chevy Nova has all the attributes of the contemporary Pro Street movement: eye-catching paint, awesome tyres and wheels, the appropriate hoodscoop and plenty of muscle (468 Chevy) to back it all up. Ramsey built the entire car single-handed and won the coveted 1st Place Pro Street award at the 1982 Car Craft Nats—when he was just 18! He is now the sole proprietor of Dan Ramsey Race Cars, located in Porter, Indiana.

ABOVE Approximately $38,000 and 3200 hours of labour have been put into Rick Dobbertin's twin-turbocharged, supercharged and nitrous oxide-injected 454-inch Pro Street Chevy Nova. Dobbertin is fortunate in that he owns a speed shop in Springfield, Virginia, and this complex piece of packaging represents a rolling billboard for that business (AA/Speed & Custom/Turbo Dynamics).

The 'Boss' era in Ford history came and went all too fast. It started in 1969 with the Boss 302 Mustang and ended in '72, the victim of government regulations and corporate politics. With a very potent, high-winding small-block, the average Boss 302 ran 0 to 60 in around 6½ seconds and clocked the quarter-mile in just under 15. It was a quick car, and there are still many people around who can appreciate its virtues. The owner of this repainted 1970 model is one of them.

BELOW Paul has done what is laughingly known as an engine transplant in his little Renault Dauphine. He's not just doubled the capacity, not even quadrupled. No, he's dropped a mill in that it is very nearly *eight times* the size of the original. What started out as an 845 cc rear-engined runabout is now a one-of-a-kind street machine with '59 Cadillac 390 cu.in. power. The front seats have been moved back a couple of feet to make way for the engine, and Paul now looks out of the rear side window and enters the car by the rear door. It certainly is weird to see this car cruising the streets with, apparently, only a guy sitting in the back and no driver!

The flanks of this lean machine are 'cobwebbed'—an age-old custom paint technique whereby long, stringy blobs of paint are spat out of the spraygun at very low pressure.

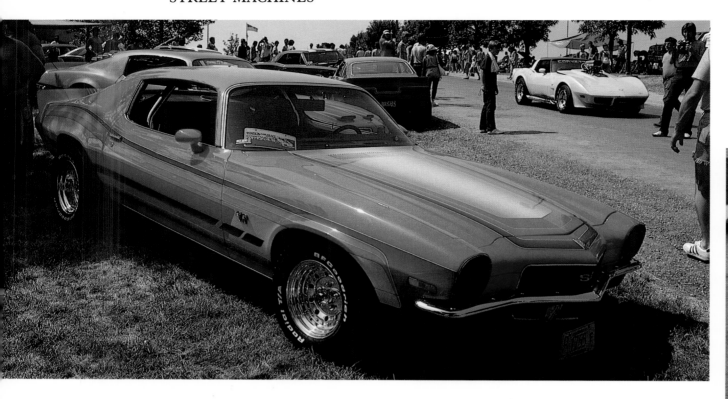

RIGHT AND BELOW Danny Taylor's '79 Malibu is late-model customising at its best. The candy-coloured masterpiece from Louisville, Kentucky, has been top-chopped 5 in., liberally louvred and dechromed, and boasts a fully hydraulic suspension system enabling the owner to alter the ride height at the flick of a switch. The tube grille, bumpers and tinted windows weren't issued at the factory, and neither was a black crushed velvet interior. Built as something of a promo vehicle for the family body'n'paint business, this low-down Chevy steals the show wherever it goes.

LEFT It's amazing what a wild paint job and a new set of wheels can do for an otherwise plain '70 Camaro. This multi-hued SS396 appeared on the cover of *Hot Rod* in July 1980. Pro custom painter Bill Carter was the man with the patience.

STREET MACHINES

BELOW Al Woodward is president of the V8 Estate Corvette Club in his home town of Detroit, so it's only fitting he should have the snazziest, most power-packin' car in the city. This '72 Vette is the proverbial 'kandy-kolored tangerine-flake streamline baby', with as much 'go' as 'show'. When he and his wife Elizabeth—the Glass Roots Racing Team—aren't doing their thing at the local dragstrip, you can be sure they're winning admiring looks on the street. Under (and largely through) the hood lies the biggest, brightest blown big-block imaginable: the motor began as a 454 Chevy and has been treated to an $\frac{1}{8}$in. overbore and a $\frac{5}{8}$in. stroker crank, which brings the capacity up to an incredible 543 cubic inches!

RIGHT Yosemite Sam, a Motown painter of national repute, demonstrated virtually *every* custom paint technique on this multi-coloured machine. The butterfly wings and some of the striping are picked out in real gold leaf, the rest is a mixture of candies and pearls.

ABOVE No shame if you didn't recognise this eight-headlight wonder as being a '74 Olds Cutlass; it's been sectioned 3 in., chopped 4 in. and lowered 5 in. There has also been about 10 in. taken out of the length, where the back seat was. Owner Bob Peterson has put some really neat tricks into his black'n'flamed custom, including electric windows, door locks, trunk lid, and even a flipdown front licence plate.

BELOW Behind Chevrolet, Ford, Pontiac and Dodge, Plymouths were the fifth most popular make of car at the 1983 Nationals. Hot-rodded Road Runner was the meanest.

ABOVE George Matulik has given a new lease of life to an old '69 Camaro. What was a 'hunkajunk' is now an eyecatching street machine with Ram Air 400 power and a velour interior. George hails from Bridgeview, Illinois.

BELOW Custom paintwork on this '69 Super Sport Camaro is early seventies style. Rear wheelarch flares are 'out' too.

In an effort to distinguish the new hi-performance Pontiac GTO from the basic model, a young engineer on the GTO committee suggested the name 'The Judge', from the popular Rowan and Martin TV show *Laugh In*. It stuck, and just over 11,000 Judge Option GTOs were manufactured from 1969 to 1971. Of these, only 357 hardtops were sold in the final production year, which explains why the owner has simply removed the hood and bolted on a supercharger. As an interesting aside, the head of that committee was one John Z. DeLorean, who 'created the GTO as a car for my own personal use . . .'

125

ABOVE Grand Rapids, Michigan's David Jackson rides herd on a 351 Boss. The original paint treatment of the '71 Mustang featured a black hood with a full-length black or silver side stripe, depending on the body colour. Just to be different, David sprayed this heavy breathing horse a misty shade of blue with red-hot flames.

RIGHT This street freak was just a harmless Ford Falcon before 'Vito's Garage' got hold of it.

BELOW Six-wheeled Jaguar XJ-S pick-up was custom-built as a promotional exercise for the 100+ International wheel company. The 30 in. body and chassis extension carries a trailing IRS, while under the bonnet lies a 'built' eight-cylinder 454 cu.in. Chevy in place of the stock V12. Four cylinders less, but double the horsepower . . .

RIGHT A convertible Impala would be most folks' idea of fun on a warm summer's evening, but some still prefer 'cruzin' in a rollcaged GTO.

129

At just 21, Andy Saunders from Poole in Dorset is probably Britain's most prolific young customiser. Several of his creations have appeared in magazines and shows right across Europe, but so far none has been as popular as this—a '68 Volvo 121 hardtop turned fifties-style kustom convertible. Quite an achievement!

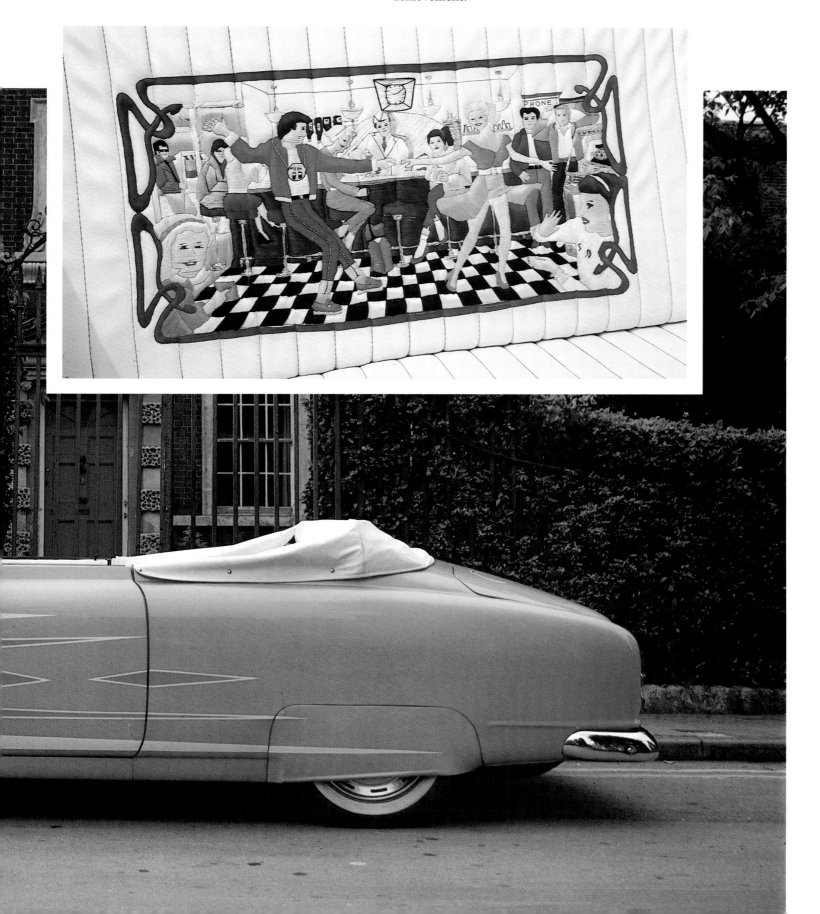

TRI-CHEVY

Chevrolet's model line-up for 1955–57 was a classic array of fine automobiles. Their styling was very much of the period: Chevy let others make idiots of themselves with fins that could fly to the Moon and chrome trim that weighed more than the engine.

For those who want the individuality of a street machine, a Tri-Chevy is a fine choice. The supply of standard vehicles to start work on is plentiful, so the price is affordable, but the results look like a million dollars.

For some, satisfaction comes from just fine-detailing everything from the upholstery to the door hinges. Others go for total customization. The engine gets a blower, new cams and the whole works that mean class-winning elimination times.

The body, too, is chopped, channelled and re-worked for a look that draws admiration from the crowd and envy from the competition.

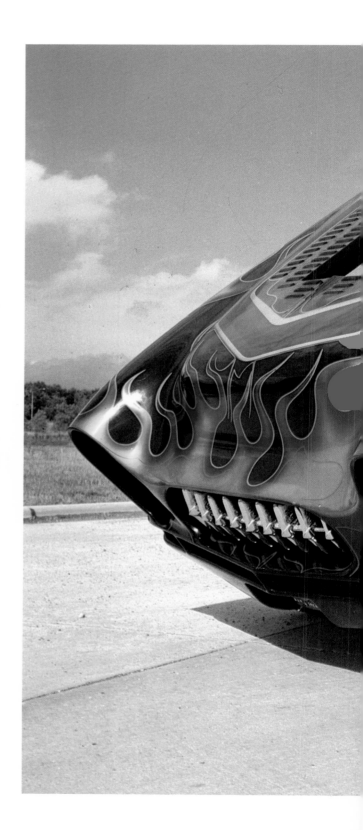

RIGHT We were looking for something 'wild' to feature and Dan Marshall's '55 Sedan Delivery really fills the bill. The top was chopped; the one-piece tilt hood has a Corvette grill and twin canted headlamps.

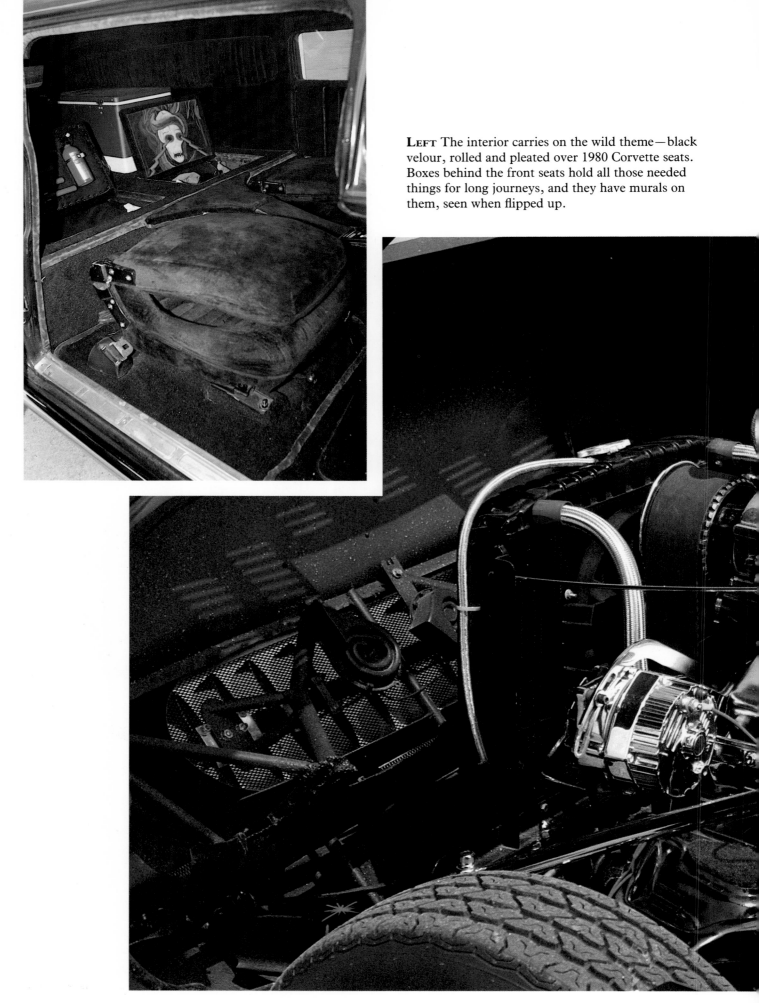

LEFT The interior carries on the wild theme—black velour, rolled and pleated over 1980 Corvette seats. Boxes behind the front seats hold all those needed things for long journeys, and they have murals on them, seen when flipped up.

BELOW With the one-piece hood flipped forward, a startling small-block Corvette engine is revealed with a gold plated 671 GMC supercharger topped off with two Holley 650s. Everything has been polished, chromed or anodised. Sitting below are many parts from a 1980 Camaro, including a set of disc brakes and steering. A Turbo 400 auto helps turn the '78 Corvette rear axle.

ABOVE '57 Bel Air under power. Good looking Sports Coupe's lines are so good, it looks as if it's flying down the road even when it's standing still.

BELOW Supercharger whine coming from John Javert's white '55. After John has passed you are left with only the fading heavy beat of a mighty V8.

RIGHT '57s are completely different from '55s and '56s. At the rear we have a pair of finned fenders; just above the rear taillight in the tailfin, driver's side, the gas cap is hidden. This '57 Bel Air two-door Sports Coupe is owned by Gene Rishforth and is one of the most collectable models today.

BELOW RIGHT '55 Bel Air complete with front fender side trim, rear fender trim, gas cap trim and lower stoneguard from wheelarch along door sill—and, of course, cruising would not be complete without the fuzzy dice.

LEFT Several things confuse the '55 and '56. This two-door Bel Air has a perfect hood bird with 'V' and badge. No 'V' on the '55 and a different bird.

BELOW Can you believe this '56 Bel Air two-door Hard Top has only 25,000 miles on the clock and that's in 28 years of motoring? We were able to find David Reid who owns this '56. He has had the car since 1976—it has the original 265 cu.in. engine which because of the 25,000 has only just been 'run in'. The whole car is original.

140

LEFT The just-right stance of Dale's Delivery was achieved by cutting two coils from the stock front suspension. The stock rear suspension is lowered by four-inch blocks between the axle and leaf springs. All trim is original '57 from across the range. Wheels are super chrome Weld Wires made with chunky spokes and covered with Eagle Goodyears. Paint is red Lipstick Enamel and is really brilliant in the US sun. Headlamps are covered with a '50's aftermarket Moons cover. The car was drag-raced for six years and held track records, thereafter in storage until eight years ago when Dale started to show it. It was 1982/83 Great Lakes Isca Division Class Champ, Custom Sedan Delivery.

BELOW LEFT Standard '57 dash, '64 Chevrolet bucket seats covered with crushed velvet in Diamond Tucked, as are the door panels, headliner and the whole of the rear. Very plush!

BELOW The styling of this one is really neat. The side trim was taken from a '57 Bel Air sedan as the original trim was just a flash from just under the door handle to the end of the fin. Dave loves louvres.

ABOVE Cecil Hall's '56 Convertible is as stock as they come, right down to wheels being of the correct pattern. The car is also equipped with a full Continental kit. Cecil, his wife and poodle enjoy cruising around. I am sure I saw the poodle drive at least once over the weekend.

BELOW The plaque in the window proclaims: Original —Unrestored, Original Paint, Original Interior, Original Chrome. Owner Frank and Vickie Orlando, Waynesburg, Ohio. 1957 four-door Sedan. What more can we say?

Above Al Hudson's immaculate '55 four-door Bel Air shows all the extras including a Continental wheel kit which could be purchased for $123. The two-tone paint was unknown before 1955 and came with the roof only, or roof, upper rear quarter and deck. Al insisted this is an original '55 Chevrolet colour scheme. 1955 saw Chevrolet launch the small-block V8—it was a high-performance, overhead-valve, lightweight engine. In all cars of this year a 'V' badge was fitted on the rear fender between the taillights and bumper.

Below Smoothed out front with tube grill in place of the eggbox, hood bird and badge have gone and lots of louvres have been punched in the hood of this '55 Bel Air sedan.

ABOVE The '55 Convertible in front started the Tri-Chevy craze and the '57 behind was the end, only one year apart, but the styling was light years away. The '57 solid red, with red and grey interior, is owned by Frank Hartmen and looks long and sleek; the '55 looks short and stocky by comparison, but the wheelbase is 115 in. on both cars. Overall length of the '55 is 195.6 in., the '57 200.

RIGHT The '57 rear was completely redesigned. Fins now appeared, and taillights at the base of the fins.

'His' and 'Hers' together. Karen Craft on the left and
Ken Craft on the right both own '55 210 Chevrolets,
far from stock.

LEFT The '55 sits really low, with the front lowered six inches and the rear five. But wait—Karen doesn't have to drive it that low and endanger the underside when grounding out: Ken installed hydraulic lifts all round so that the car can have sufficient ground clearance when required. Ken completed the chassis work and the bodywork, and he painted it in '79 Chev red. Chromestar wires shod with Goodyear radials with raised white letters and Lakes pipes plus pinstriping finishes the car in fine style.

BELOW LEFT The interior has the neat theme too. The upholstery was by D&F Upholstery and is done in red crushed velvet with gold buttons and braid as contrast.

Carpets are the same colour and a neat finishing touch. Stock dash with pin striping, red and white 'teardrop' knobs for radio and switches. Steering is a '67 Pontiac tilt. The two small toggle switches projecting from the base of the seat are for the hydraulic lifts.

BELOW 327 cu.in. small-block is equipped with modified 270 heads and an ESK cam and Mallory ignition system. Headman headers get rid of the spent gases. The most visible part of the engine is the six Holleys on an Offenhauser manifold, topped with individual chrome air cleaners. Gearbox is the all-trusty 3-speed Turbo 350 auto.

LEFT The black acrylic enamel paint applied by Ken is complemented by the blue crushed velvet in a diamond tuft pattern. The front seats are Monte Carlo and they swivel; the rear 'wrapround' back seat is made from a Ford T-bird. Stock dash is set off with '50s 'teardrop' switch knobs, as in Karen's, but black and white. Steering wheel is '67 Cadillac and tilts. Ken has a body shop called Woody's in Centerburg, Ohio.

RIGHT Ken's '55 has much more in body modifications than Karen's. He carried out all the bodywork, first chopping the top by four inches, then lowering the front six inches and the rear five, giving a low mean look. The hood is stuffed with louvres and a custom tube grille replaces the stock eggbox grille. The hood bird ornament and badge have been removed to clean up the front. Pinstriping and Appleton spotlights give the 'custom' look.

BELOW RIGHT The rear of Ken's '55 has had the 'custom' treatment with the removal of the badge, key and licence plate and also the little 'V' badges on the end of the fenders (if this car had had a V8 when built in 1955). Super pinstriping is around the radio aerial and rear lights and, to give it a finishing touch, a pair of 1950s aftermarket Lee lenses.

RIGHT *Midnite Delite* was a major award winner at the Columbus Classic Chevy Convention. The chop job of four inches gives the car a mean look. No external door handles as the locks work on electric solenoids, vertical trim to the belt line dip has been taken away and Lakes pipes have been installed under door sills. Hydraulic rams have been installed at the front end. Appliance wires with Goodyear radials finish it off. Under the hood is a similar setup to Karen's—327 cu.in. Chevy small-block Duntof cam, Power Pack heads, Tube headers, Mallory ignition and Offenhauser manifold with six Holley carbs.

TRI-CHEVY

BELOW These Continental kits held the spare wheel, giving some extra room in the trunk. Martin Coones says this is a genuine GM accessory: he bought it himself and fitted it to the '57 in the picture. Not being able to leave anything standard, Martin fitted the gold grille and removed the Chevrolet word badge and centralised the 'V'. He has also doubled up on the rear lights by fitting another light in the bumper where the reversing light was; all taillights carry blue dots.

RIGHT First thing that strikes you about Larry Fullerton's 1955 Hard Top is the candy paint over the black lacquer. Candy paint like this was a big thing a few years back and it is nice to see a '55 with such paint still around. It was painted by Harvey Scott. The car was brought back from California by a friend of Larry's and the original cost was $500, not as much as the 1955 price of around $2000. Larry has owned the car since 1968 and has owned two other '55s. We have a hint of what is under the hood with the external rev counter and scoop for more air and clearance. To clean up the front the badge and hood bird have been removed, as has the stainless vertical trim just past the door pillar.

153

ABOVE Black diamond pleated interior of Larry's '55 was sewn up by Ambassador House in traditional hot-rod theme. The stock dash has more gauges than the original, all monitoring the engine internals when drag racing; the stock steering wheel was swapped for one from a Chevrolet Impala.

RIGHT Larry is a truck driver who likes to drag-race his '55. The basis of the engine is a Chevy small-block, 302 cu.in. with a Racer Brown roller cam and a pair of Chevy 202 heads. To pump the gas in he installed a Weiand Tunnel Ram inlet manifold and, to top this off, two Holley 660s—hence the hood scoop. The whole engine and bay are finished with lots of chrome and stainless braided lines; Mallory Msd ignition lights the gas and Hooker headers help get rid of it. All this horsepower is passed through a Doug Nash five-speed manual gearbox, through a 'strange' driveshaft to a Dana 600 axle.

154

BELOW Fine stance: Firestone slicks on Cragar chrome wheels, biggies on the rear and skinnies on the front, in the true drag-racing style.

LEFT This 1956 Chevy Sedan Delivery was of very high quality but we could not find the owner to get more information. It is an excellent example, possibly the second Delivery the guy has built, and runs a blower under the air intake and dual Holley carbs.

BELOW 1957 Sedan Delivery 150. This very neat Delivery was smooth in its lines, the back being more upright than the Nomad of that year. Less than 10,000 were produced.

BELOW RIGHT Continental kit exposed on this '57. Putting the spare tyre outside the trunk obviously gives you more inside.

BOTTOM RIGHT The trunk is shaved (Chevy badge and large 'V' taken off) on Dale Egle's '57 210 Sedan, named *Poison Ivy*. Organic green candy apple over black pearl paint. Super pinstriping too. Dale and his wife are two neat people and the car is one of the best.

Mike Holderman, a welder at General Motors, found his '57 Chevy ten years ago in La Fontaine, his home town in Indiana; the purchase price was a mere $250 dollars. Construction time was nine years which shows in the overall quality. Mike carried out all the work on the car apart from the upholstery. Body modifications are shaved hood and trunk and 198 louvres were punched into the hood!

ABOVE Neat and immaculate—what other words can describe the '57 engine bay? Hours have been spent getting all the parts in the right place. 350 small-block, L46 cam, 327/350 heads, Offenhauser inlet with two

Holleys, Black Jack headers playing the V8 burble into turbo mufflers and just everything is polished or chrome-plated. Gearbox is a 450 turbo with a B&M shift kit.

RIGHT Mike is proud of his '57 and rightly so—many hours' work and it's never trailered. The rear licence plate has been frenched into the trunk and the door handles are flush type from a Grand Prix. Mike also applied the very striking paint using Candy Brandywine over Gold, Pearl and shadow flames. Neat note on the trunk says 'Baby you know what I like'.

ABOVE All Nomads were Bel Airs. This sparkling example, owned by Robert Sykona, was a newly restored car; he was fitting the windscreen at midnight, the night before the Classic Chevy weekend. No wonder these Nomads are sought after, with only 8530 cars built in 1955. They are particularly pretty and it's amazing that something so good-looking sold so badly. *Motor Trend* in late '55 gave it third place in their 'Most aesthetically styled' contest for '55, with Chrysler and Ford in front.

ABOVE RIGHT The side trim varies on '57s. The 150 has a horizontal bar along the rear fender and vertical to the belt line dip; the 210 and Bel Air have trim as you see in this photo; 210's have the forward pointing 'triangle' painted on two-tone paint schemes with the second colour (obviously on a solid colour car it was painted with the same colour). On the Bel Air, Harley Earl designed a brushed aluminium panel with the Bel Air badge in gold.

RIGHT Look at the racer on the next spread and then at this '56 210 and you can see the difference between it and Bel Air trim.

BELOW A fine example of a 1956 150 rebuilt by Martin West of Brentford, England, with all original trim apart from the side trim which should continue from the vertical belt line dip to the rear bumper. A stock 350 Chevy was installed apart from a Holley carb and headers, Hayes clutch to keep contact between the 350 and Muncie four-speed manual. A set of sparkling chrome Cragar S/S wheels of 6 × 14 front, 7 × 15 rear, contrast well with the black paint. Other goodies help the ride—with Gabriel air shocks and traction bars on the rear and Red Ride shocks on the front. Cherry Bombs hold that lovely V8 burble.

RIGHT The driver of this '56 drag racer could have been either Mr Kincaid or Mr Hartman. He was driving from a Friday night meet to a Saturday night meet and was passing close to the Classic Chevy Convention so he decided to call in. We did gather that the car travelled the quarter-mile in 12.80 sec. and finished at 106 mph. The engine is the ever excellent 350 with a centre squirt carburettor.

BELOW RIGHT '57 Nomads were trimmed the same as the Bel Air with brushed aluminium in the 'triangle' and gold capped front fender louvres. The ribbed roof was common to all three Nomad models, the only special exterior trim having the Nomad script on the tailgate and a small gold 'V' on V8 powered models. Few of 'The Wagon with the Sports Car Flair' were sold in 1957.

LEFT Silver metallic paint on this '57 Bel Air Sports Coupe gives an original look, even down to a set of original wheels with 215-70-14 tyres. A Chevy 350 with a 350 Turbo from a '71 Chevy helps turn those wheels; the engine is just cleaned up with M/T rocker covers and chrome air cleaner. All the brakes and running gear are stock and that's how Dave Hartshorne wants it, now wanting only to add whitewalls.

ABOVE Two-tone paint, a little different. Harry Blunden owns this super '57 four-door Bel Air. Most of the running gear is all-original as are all the trim parts. A small-block has been equipped with a Holley, Edelbrock inlet and Black Jack headers with Cherry Bomb mufflers.

BELOW Black and flames are always a sign of a hot rod. Simon Davies' 1957 150 has all the classic signs with deep black paint and orange, white and red flames, pinstriping in white and a set of American racing wheels, five-spoke with spinners. Under the hood is the first choice, a 327 backed up by a Turbo 400 running through to the original rear axle, supported by leaf springs and air shocks. A pair of '69 Camaro discs are in front to bring up the braking efficiency. Interior has been re-upholstered in deep-buttoned, brilliant wine red dralon.

ABOVE 1955 Chevy Sedan dash. The basic design was used in all models 150, 210 and Bel Air, but this slightly customised interior includes extra gauges, radio cassette, CB and tilt steering column and, of course, a set of fluffy dice.

RIGHT A neat rear-end interior, clean and, of course, non-stock.

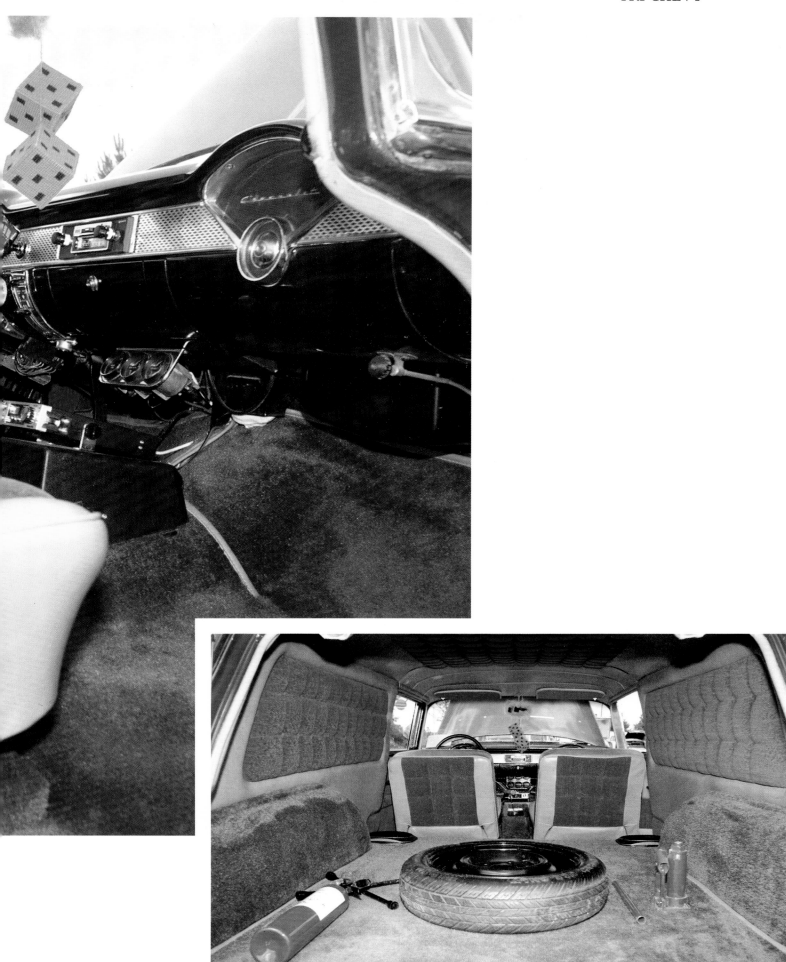

168

ABOVE LEFT Here we see an original '56 dash, with central glove compartment and original design seat cloth and vinyl trim. David Reid owns this fine example.

ABOVE This is as stock as you will see. Cecil Hall's '56 Convertible has a dash with double hump laid out in a similar way to the '55; quite different, though, in that the 'bow ties' have been swapped for an oblong design.

LEFT The dash design was completely altered for '57. Instruments are now clustered around the speedo, and lights are used for oil and amps. The dash still houses the central glove compartment. Steering wheel is also original; spot light rear-view mirror is an aftermarket accessory and can be adjusted from inside the car. This '57 is owned by Cindy and Dick Brown.

BELOW LEFT Here is one at last, a little old small-block. This 265 in David Reid's '56 is as original as you will see with only 25,000 miles on it. The small-block from 265 through 350 is such a neat design. All can be fitted with a variety of gearboxes. Long live the small-block!

LEFT 235 cu.in. six in Ruth Anderson's unrestored '56. This is as stock as they come. 125 hp at 4000 rpm with a single barrel and three-speed Powerglide.

BELOW Take your basic 235 cu.in. six-cylinder, bolt on dual carbs, hot cam, balance and blueprint and you have a hot little mover. Then drop it into, say, a '55 Bel Air and add dual pipes. Then go racing.

EXOTICA ITALIANA

Not all the action on American streets is home-grown. The Europeans are capable of some pretty awesome exercises in style. But with the Lamborghinis, the designers just knew the Miura, Jalpa, Countach and all the other fine automobiles would soon find a welcome in the USA.

Many high-class Italian models have been directly influenced by the United States. Ford V8s powered De Tomaso's Pantera and some beautiful Maseratis. Even Ferrari has made cars that had the USA in mind. The Superamericas immediately won applause when they were landed in New York.

The engines, too, were made for the United States. The Lamborghini powerplants all have special equipment that meets the Federal regulations. Many other details are different. They may look Italian but they are American at heart.

RIGHT Very busy with a Countach, two Miuras and two Espadas in view. What makes better sense than to have your car serviced at the factory which built it, possibly even by the same staff who actually built it?

Simply beautiful Miura SV owned by Peter Oates and superbly restored by Graypaul Motors near Loughborough (usually known for their Ferrari work). For some enthusiasts still the most striking and technically interesting Lamborghini ever made.

The original technical and styling design of the Miura was unquestionably inspired by the Ford GT-40. Gianpaolo Dallara readily admits that he saw the need for a mid-engined monocoque in the general style of that famous Ferrari race track challenger.

Miura SV means the last series, after the P400 and the S, dated around 1971/72. Approximately 150 of this last series were made, with 475 of the Miura P400 and 140 of the S.

RIGHT What should have by rights been a Porsche 911 and Ferrari 246/308 Dino beater, wasn't. The early Urraco couldn't stand the pace, although to be fair, it wasn't all their own fault. Today, they are beginning to be seen as highly desirable mid-engine sports cars. Transverse mid-V8-engine Berton bodied Urraco was handsome and could be fast; build quality and delivery were suspicious. This is an early P250 model (because of its large double vent on the front panel) fitted with some later parts such as the road wheels.

LEFT Engine maintenance is difficult on all Lamborghinis, and the Urraco is no exception. This shot clearly shows the closeness of the transverse V8 engine to the passengers' seat backs.

BELOW The Jalpa runs a 3.5-litre version of the 90-degree double overhead camshaft V8—quoted 255 hp. Lovely road test car at speed; chassis number ZA9J00000 ELA 12150, engine number 12150.

RIGHT Silhouette—a rare beast indeed. Cruelly it could be called a Urraco P300 with a Targa top. Reality says something else—it was much more. First shown in March 1976, the Urraco 3000 had been restyled in a most aggressive way with new wheels, 'square' wheelarches, new rear side window treatment and an air dam. Only 52 cars were made.

EXOTICA ITALIANA

BELOW The most outrageous production car in the world—the Countach. This one is a 5000 S. S production started in 1979 after 160 cars had already been made between 1974 and 1977; the 5-litre engine came in late 1982. Gull-wing style doors require clever mechanicals. Countach rear wing is an optional extra, though one is usually fitted.

BELOW Countach around town. Docile the car can be too: high-speed driving and round-town slowness both come easily to its mechanicals provided you remember it's a large car.

BOTTOM A Countach S, a late second-series S with colour-coded rear wing and Bravo-style wheels and P7 Pirelli tyres. The S still carried over the LP400, 3929 cc dohc V12 engine—5 litres came with the S 5000.

BELOW Beautiful, longitudinally mounted double overhead camshaft V12 is mid-engined but the gearbox is actually under the gear lever inside the cockpit, without pulleys or cables. A driveshaft goes effectively through the sump of the engine to the differential at the other end, to the rear of the car.

LEFT Countach interior. Its style is certainly in keeping with the car's exterior. Anyone who's ridden in a Countach will know how gripping those seats need to be.

BELOW The 5000 S, the model just prior to the latest Quattrovalvole, with covers open. For the test driver, just everyday; for us, perhaps much more.

Jalpa, today's other Lamborghini. Like the Countach's, its current bodyshell design has been developed from something not quite the same, although, unlike the Countach, this one is pretty far removed from the original, the Urraco P250 in 1972. Obviously the Countach of 1971 was right to start with. The Jalpa is the affordable Lamborghini but undoubtedly suffers under the shadow of the Countach, simply because the Countach is so radical and so exotic. Jalpa drivers all tell of the same excellent road manners.

OFF ROAD

Off-road driving caught alight with the Jeep. Originally designed for the armed forces during World War Two, the go-anywhere 'battle taxi' showed everyone what fun it was to come off the highway and head up quiet tracks.

Some use their 4 × 4s for fishing trips, hunting, or just going to that spot where a cookout can be enjoyed in superb, natural surroundings. For others, the rugged, competitive approach is the only type of off-road driving that satisfies. Off-roading builds self-reliance, skill and an appreciation for the environment.

Whether it is a specially adapted 4 × 4 for river, swamp or mountain events, America has an expert who can make or modify virtually anything. Provided the basic vehicle is strong, it can be made stronger to withstand the rigours of the wild. And off-roading gives the stylist the excuse, if an excuse were necessary, to give bodywork a look that proclaims the 4 × 4's real character even when stationary in a mall parking lot.

RIGHT 1968 Chevy El Camino ('caratruck') sits on Blazer running gear. Owner Steve Goeglein spent many hours perfecting this one. Pikes Peak landscape is spectacular.

Above Dodge L6 four-wheel drive truck of 1958, the first year with the quad headlamps. Part of the top grille is missing. Dodge had special tough vehicle status left over from the Second World War.

Above right Obviously not yet finished—some critics might even say that the 4WD conversion to this '57 Chevy Nomad (2-door estate) should never have begun. Door must have come from another model—trim doesn't match.

Right Still a leader in small four-wheel drivers, Fuji Heavy Industries decided America needed a pickup. Hence the Brat. Bed-mounted seats use the cab as a backrest. Appreciating the low underbody clearance, Subarus score. Azusa Canyon lake.

BELOW Light weight and good traction avoid the need for four-wheel drive in this desert terrain. The ubiquitous VW supplies most of the parts for this rail. The steering comes from a Ford Pinto—few like the VW 'box'.

BELOW Sun, shadow and dust. Stock Toyota Hilux
4 × 4 fooling around.

ABOVE LEFT Nelly's Ford Bronco with the faithful 302-inch V8 aboard. This must be an early Bronco (first introduced in 1965). The snow confirms it's Pikes Peak, Colorado.

LEFT Spectator park at Pikes Peak. This F-series Ford pickup shows off American life—cowboy hat, beer can and 'chocolate chip cookie' bag!

ABOVE Although on Virginian plates, this stock CJ7 Renegade Jeep is at Old Tucson, Arizona. V8 power makes it one of America's most costly to insure.

195

LEFT Swamp buggy racing—wheels mostly on the deck—gets popular. Here, at Naples in the Everglades in South Florida, various jeeps seem to work.

BELOW Waterproofing is obviously essential for this game. No mean task. Each driver/passenger seems to have different ideas as to how deep the swamp is. Naples, Florida.

LEFT A standard, factory-supplied paint scheme on a Ford Bronco, shot in Manitou Springs, Colorado. Black paint can't be good for the temperature inside the vehicle. Air conditioning usually sorts it out.

RIGHT Just a fun truck although without four-wheel drive. Very stock Chevrolet 'big' pickup on the Arizona Highway in the Apache Mountains.

BELOW The flat-windscreen Chevy-Van of 1964. Came as standard with either a 90 hp four or 120 hp six, plus 2WD. This understated red van comes out of the Azusa mud hole with V8 and 4WD transplant.

199

LEFT Water and mud must play hell with diff seals and brakes, let alone the clutch. Ford with winch about to haul Chevy without. Breaking strain of the cable must be at least 5000 lb. Heavy work.

BELOW LEFT It appears that enthusiasts have dug this hole especially to get stuck in. Once again the winch ensures none ever lose their trucks altogether. Twist on that pickup is frightening.

BELOW Jacked-up and mildly customised. This short F-100 (6½-foot Cargo box with 117-inch wheelbase) Ford is built just for fun—here, at Azusa Canyon. Paint is more elaborate than factory's Tu-Tone.

BELOW Keen off-road new car sales lot. This man sells Ford and Jeep at Dana Point, on the Pacific Coast Highway in California. Ford F-150 Ranger has Regular Cab, a Styleside bed of 6¾ feet.

BELOW CENTRE Storm brewing over Colorado Springs. Chrysler/Dodge dealer has pinstriped Ramcharger with whitewall tyres, nerf bar and rollbar-mounted driving lamps—no off-road tyres yet.

BELOW RIGHT Ford's F Series 'Freewheeling Flareside' (their stepside) with truck style customising. One-way mural, stacks, cab step, door trim, rollbar, wheelarch flares, wheels and finally paint.

RIGHT The Ford F series is very popular. Here's a near-new F-250 Regular Cab but with 8-foot Styleside Cargo box. Datsun is 1981 King Cab 4WD. Azusa Canyon.

204

LEFT Conversions of this sort are common. The engineering has to be sound. So many components are currently available to do this that little will need to be custom-made. Late '40s panel truck bodyshell is cute on this 1949 Chevy.

BELOW Down Pikes Peak after it's all over for the spectators. First vehicle is the Chevy Styleline, a light panel truck cum Sedan Delivery equipped with 4WD, second is 1957 Chevrolet Nomad, third a Jeep.

ABOVE LEFT Passenger enjoyed his burger. Typical everyday highway scene (on the way to Albuquerque). Well used Ford F-series 4WD pickup is specially raised on its suspension for soft off-roading.

ABOVE Toyota feast: resting at Azusa Canyon enjoying the sun. Left to right: Land Cruiser FJ40 (a diesel engine would have made it a BJ40); Hilux 4 × 4 mini pickup, well modified; Hilux 4 × 4, new and stock.

LEFT Not yet downsized, this recent 'full-size' Chevy near Oceanside, CA, still runs a 305-inch V8. Wheels are special, the rest is stock. Unlike the Jeep's door mirrors, you look at them through the door window.

ABOVE Anything goes. This split-screen Microbus has the familiar huge cutouts for oversize rear tyres. Because it's essentially Beetle a lot of suitable equipment is available to increase its off-road capability. Azusa Canyon again.

ABOVE A Baja Bug using a kit. Note the roof oil cooler
(back) and driving lights (front). Rear screen is
punched out. Azusa Canyon watering hole,
California's interior.

OFF ROAD

BELOW Delightful Pikes Peak shot. Approaching the Devil's Playground on the way up is Danny Arant in his home-built Grizzly VW. Obvious is the different thinking in chassis design as to the perfect dirt-surface hillclimber.

RIGHT Another Beetle made in Southern California. This bright Baja Bug hasn't been radically altered, in fact. Most of it bolts on. This beauty will go best on the Coast Highway on which it sits, not the desert.

BELOW RIGHT The VW 181 Thing built in Mexico but seen here in Encinatas, California. Conceived when the off-road scene was growing as a sort of modern *Kubelwagen*. This one has nonstock wheels. Off-road capability: nil.

ABOVE LEFT VW flat-four power in this Pikes Peak hillclimber: Canadian Bill Warner spits dust in his 1975 Newman Dreager VW sponsored by Sunshine Rentals. Built for the job.

LEFT Home-produced, but one of many, this VW sand rail uses a VW 1600 'upright fan' motor. Husband-and-wife team run in the desert near Ocotillo, close to the Mexican border in California. It's very hot.

ABOVE So hot, the canal looks like tarmac. Here at Glamis, near Mexicali, an umbrella helps only a little. Paddle sand rear tyres dominate this VW-powered rail. The event here was cancelled; it was too hot.

213

RIGHT 'Beach Boys'—Pismo Beach in CA is one of the last dunes areas which can still be used, or abused, by off-roaders however laid-back. Note smiles.

BELOW CJ6 at Azusa Canyon. The dried up river bed provides an ideal playpark for such vehicles. Goodyear Wrangler R/T tyres complement wide aftermarket 'mags'.

ABOVE British Jeep racer appropriately called *Black Power*. This Willys has Daimler power with its 2½-litre push rod V8. The jump is on the tank range at Aldershot, home of the British Army. Rare UK-registered Land Cruiser in the background.

LEFT Mobile shoe shop via Ebis, the Philippines. Selling flip flops. Perhaps the stack on the hood front helps to compensate for the enormous rear overhang.

BELOW Filipino bus park. Manila streets, and elsewhere, are crowded with some 27,000 Jeepneys. First built by Mr Clod Delfino from an American Army leftover Willys; today they are custom-built.

ABOVE A handsome factory-painted blue and white Dodge Power Ram. V8 power is fun but is getting too expensive to run. These large pickups are now losing sales to the mini pickups.

ABOVE RIGHT Antique wrecker in Cripple Creek. It's still being used. It's a four-wheel drive 1939 Ford '1-tonner' with 85 horsepower and hydraulic brakes (the first year). This one comes with a plate stating 'Marmon-Herrington All Wheel Drive'. Rust is not so damaging in America's south-west.

RIGHT Ford's Jeep equivalent comes not from their often two-wheel drive F series but as the Bronco. This XLT custom pack treatment is pretty common now. Little off-road work for this one, though.

Left Front plates are not obligatory in California. Front grille and headlamps suggests that this is a 1978 Ford Custom (more comfortable Ford Ranger with Mohave embossed vinyl seat trim!). Actually another F-100 Regular Cab with Styleside bed.

Below left International Scout from International Harvester better known for agricultural equipment, perhaps. This one is modified and difficult to date accurately. California.

Below Two-door Jeep Cherokee Chief (5900 cc V8, 3-speed auto QuadraTrac, and a kerb weight of 3858 lb). Shop's called Suzette.

Bottom Chevy Van custom-converted to four-wheel drive. Big winch protrudes in front of the grille but behind the nerf bar. Anyone stuck knows the strength of a good winch.

BELOW Real swamp buggy in the Everglades. Florida. Is it a boat?

RIGHT Off-road fun can come with two-wheel drive and cheaply. Honda's 248 cc motocross (not yet water-cooled for the Odyssey) has plenty of horsepower for everyday Azusa Canyon. If you have the strength, and courage, there is nowhere you can't go. Hot-rod versions are around. Help!

BELOW RIGHT 1981 spec. Odyssey comes in red instead of yellow (usually), full rollcage, headlamp, and improved suspension. Honda says 'As far as you can get from sensible transportation . . .' Three-wheeler in the background is Honda's ATC.

Purpose-built off-road racing buggy, made in the USA
but seen here at Bordon in the UK.